Passive Income Online

20 Ideas and Strategies to Start an Online Business that Makes a Passive Income for You Every Day.

© Copyright 2017 Connection Books Club
All Rights Reserved.

This document is presented with the desire to provide reliable, quality information about the topic in question and the facts discussed within. This Book is sold under the assumption that neither the publisher or the author should be asked to provide the services discussed within. If any discussion, professional or legal, is otherwise required a proper professional should be consulted.

The reproduction, duplication or transmission of any of the included information is considered illegal whether done in print or electronically. Creating a recorded copy or a secondary copy of this work is also prohibited unless the action of doing so is first cleared through the Publisher and condoned in writing. All rights reserved.

Any information contained in the following pages is considered accurate and truthful and that any liability through inattention or by any use or misuse of the topics discussed within falls solely on the reader. There are no cases in which the Publisher of this work can be held responsible or be asked to provide reparations for any loss of monetary gain or other damages which may be caused by following the presented information in any way shape or form.

The following information is presented purely for informative purposes and is therefore considered universal. The information presented within is done so without a contract or any other type of assurance as to its quality or validity.

Any trademarks which are used are done so without consent and any use of the same does not imply consent or permission was gained from the owner. Any trademarks or brands found within are purely used for clarification purposes and no owners are in anyway affiliated with this work.

Table of Contents

Introduction 1
Fulfillment by Amazon 4
eBay Arbitrage 6
Dollar Store Arbitrage 8
Affiliate Marketing via Blogging 10
Affiliate Marketing via Facebook 12
Affiliate Marketing via YouTube 14
Create a Webinar 16
Sell Stock Photos 18
Use Your Smartphone 20
Create Evergreen Written Content 22
Become an Instagram Personality 24
Become a YouTube Personality 26
Become a Facebook Personality 28
Peer-to-Peer Real Estate Investment 30
Other Types of Peer to Peer Lending 32
Run a Comparison Site 34
Run a Lead Capture Site 36
Run a Website that Sells a Real-World Service 38
Run a Drop Shipping Business 40
Organize Public Domain Information 42
Wrap up: Passive Income overview 47

Introduction

Congratulations on downloading *Passive Income: 20 Ideas and Strategies to Start an Online Business That Make a Passive Income for You Every* Day and thank you for doing so. The reality of the 9 to 5 job being enough to support most people is becoming more and more of a myth with each passing year. As such, finding the right passive income stream for you is the right choice to ensure economic stability in the long term. In each chapter, you will discover the internet secrets that has allowed thousands of people to earn lots of money.

You can analyze each one of these 20 wonderful money streams with this book. All of them are big opportunities. Choose the one that is best for you! With today`s technology we have the opportunity to start an online business and work from home, and still have a lot of time to spend with our family. This book has valuable information, that you can use to start your own online business, or to implement it, in your current one.

The following chapters will discuss 20 different potential scenarios you could implement to generate a real passive income stream, if you pursue it to fruition. This book is a big step forward towards getting you started down the path that seems the most profitable for you, if you hope to find the success described within you are going to have to start out with as much information as possible. Remember, knowledge is power.

Every effort was made to ensure it is full of as much useful information as possible, please enjoy!

Thank you for your purchase of this eBook! I hope you enjoy reading this eBook as much as I enjoyed writing it. As part of your purchase, I invite you to join my email subscribers. This FREE subscription lets you receive a newsletter, highlighting the great new books available from Connection Books Club and other exclusive business and self development information. Subscribing is easy, and members receive great deals and fantastic eBooks at a discount! All you need to do is click this link to enter your email:

http://www.connectionbooksclub.com/bonus/

In addition to this great opportunity to subscribe to incredible discounts and our newsletter, as a welcome gift, you'll receive a FREE eBook download! Learn how to secure your financial future with the informative eBook, *Money Management: Learn How to Organize Your Financial Life and Invest in Your Future*. It's yours for FREE once you've enrolled!

http://www.connectionbooksclub.com/bonus/

Welcome to the club, and we hope you enjoy your purchase as well as our FREE welcome gift!

Have you ever wished that you were better with money?

Do you ever find yourself being overwhelmed by the state of your personal finances?

Would you like to become more financially responsible?

Now you can, with **5 Reasons to Invest in Money Management: Learn How to Organize Your Financial**

Life and Invest in Your Future, a short self-help book that is packed with information on how to make the most of your financial situation.

If you want to be able to lower your interest rates, learn up to date money management strategies and turn your financial situation into one of prosperity and stability, then you'll find the answers inside, with solid advice that includes:

- **Strategies which are designed for the average person**
- **Your options for retirement**
- **Hacks for navigating the grocery store's subtle spending traps**
- **Ways to pay less than you owe on credit cards and other outstanding debts**
- **Finding freedom with financial stability**

Suitable for complete novices, **5 Reasons to Invest in Money Management** is a book that will transform the way you look at and deal with your finances.

Download a free copy and start investing in your future today! http://www.connectionbooksclub.com/bonus/

Prosperity is waiting for **YOU**!

Fulfillment by Amazon

Fulfillment by Amazon is a type of retail arbitrage that allows you to purchase items you feel you might be able to make a profit from before sending them to Amazon who then takes care of storage and order fulfillment and sends you a check, minus their cut for the trouble, twice each month. Retail arbitrage is simply a fancy word for buying items on the cheap and selling them for a profit later on and it has really taken off in the past decade thanks to an ever increasing reliance by the public on online shopping solutions.

What sets the Fulfillment by Amazon option apart from other types of retail arbitrage is that those who sell their products through the program receive preferential treatment in a number of interesting ways. The first is that their items will be listed ahead of any similar item that are not part of the fulfillment program. Perhaps most importantly however, everything you sell as a Fulfilment by Amazon member is eligible for free shipping thanks to the free shipping promise that comes with every Amazon Prime membership.

Taken together these two factors will ensure that your products are picked over those from sellers who are interested in going it on their own virtually every single time, even if the competition offers better prices and still offers free shipping. The 2 day or less guarantee is simply going to be too much to pass up in almost every scenario. Fulfillment by Amazon does also have a $40 per month fee as well as the percentage taken of every sale, however, so if you are going to commit to this passive income opportunity you will want to send them plenty of high margin items each month, as well as post them to your store page, in order to ensure you are not simply throwing money out of the window.

After signing up for the program you will want to download the Amazon Seller application which will let you scan the barcode of any item you are potentially interested in selling to find out several interesting pieces of information. It will show you how many different stores are currently selling the item, if Amazon itself is selling the item, and how much you would make off the item if you sold it right now after all relevant fees have been subtracted. It also shows you how popular that particular item is in its relevant category so you have a realistic idea of how long it might take the item in question to sell if the current trend persists.

When it comes time to find items to sell, the rookie retail arbitrage mistake is to go for a small number of expensive items so you don't need to pay extensive storage fees in return for a larger profit. This is a risky proposition; however, as these items could just as easily sit for weeks or months without any movement, causing you to essentially pay a monthly fee to watch your items not sell. Instead, the better choice is to find a good deal on every item such as ink cartridges or cleaning supplies. Not only are these items simple to ship to Amazon, you are almost guaranteed a much faster turnaround time.

eBay Arbitrage

If you like the sound of retail arbitrage but don't want to actually go to the trouble of finding physical items, then eBay arbitrage might be more your style. In eBay Arbitrage instead of finding products that you might be able to sell in the real world, you instead search eBay.com for items that are selling at a higher price than they are currently also selling for on Amazon.com. You then take advantage of this disparity, minus fees, and either buy the item off of Amazon and send it to the winner of your eBay auction or simply purchase the item via Amazon and then having them ship the item as a gift to the eBay auction winner (frowned upon by Amazon).

When it comes to finding the right items to perform this type of arbitrage with on the regular, the first thing you will want to do is find the right niche for you. For starters, you will always want to avoid electronics as Asian companies are going to be unquestionably able to provide these items at a lower price, every single time. Instead, the best way to find a good niche is to choose a category and take a look at the completed listings that come up as well. You want to find a niche that has enough sales to provide a brisk turnover without resorting to one which is already stuffed with individual sellers.

After finding the right niche, all that is really left for you to do is keep an eye on the listings on Amazon and wait to post to eBay until the prices swing in your favor. A great way to chart the prices of items over the long term is through the website CamelCamelCamel.com which shows the general price a specific item has been selling for over a specified period of time. This makes it a great tool if you are unsure if you have found an item that is a great deal or if its price has just slowly decreased over time.

When posting items to eBay it is important to never post more than one or two at a time. Seeing a large number of similar items all readily available mitigates the item's perceived scarcity which will make it less likely that buyers will pay top dollar for your items. Additionally, it is important to fill out each listing as completely as possible and make an effort to make the item seem as attractive to potential buyers as possible. Additionally, keeping the number of duplicate items you post to a minimum protects you from losing your investment if the cost of the item in question suddenly rises on Amazon.

While participating in eBay arbitrage it is important to always be comparing prices to ensure that you are not accidentally cutting into your profits by not listing with current market trends. While doing so, however, it is important to not get so caught up in finding the best deals that you fail to actually list items regularly. Stick with your niche and you will find the amount of research required will drop off drastically after the initial learning curve.

Dollar Store Arbitrage

Dollar store arbitrage is a form of online retail arbitrage that specifically focuses on creating bundles of items from common goods found at the dollar store in a way that significantly increases the value of the items as a whole. Retail arbitrage is a successful venture because people are willing to pay a little extra for convenience, especially if they find you are offering a group of items that would be even more time consuming for them to assemble themselves.

When focusing on dollar store arbitrage it is important to understand that many of the items you will find there are manufactured specifically for those locations which mean that many people will never come into contact with the items you are selling in any other instance. This means that items which feature the type of licensed character that is never going to go out of style (think Disney, Marvel or DC characters and Star Wars) are always going to be worth something eventually, even if you have to wait for the available stock of the items to dry up first.

When it comes to items like coloring books, puzzles or games featuring the right type of characters, you can either follow the bundling processed outlined below, or consider these items a long term investment and wait a year or more for their value to mature. At that point you can guarantee that a parent whose child is obsessed with the character in question will pay $10 or more for a $1 coloring book just because it is one their child has not already consumed in its entirety. In these instances, it is important you consider storage possibilities as you wouldn't want to store an item with Amazon for that long if you hoped to make any money back on it.

If you are instead interested in a faster turnaround, albeit one that offers less dramatic returns, then your best choice is to buy a variety of similarly themed items or many different items featuring the same licensed character and group them together to create a greater amount of perceived value. Customers are much more willing to pay $20 for 5 different puzzles featuring Disney characters than they are to pay $5 for a single puzzle, especially if you are selling your items via a fulfillment by Amazon option. When creating these bundles it is important to try and create as many of the same bundle as possible to mitigate the costs in creating a unique barcode or the bundle which is described below.

Creating a barcode is a simple process and there are numerous websites including BarcodesTalk.com which will create one for you practically automatically. It doesn't come without a cost, however, and at around $10 per barcode, you will cut into your profit margins surprisingly quickly if you focus on creating on 1 or 2 copies of a bundle instead of 10 or 20. From there it is only a matter of posting the item as normal.

Enjoying your eBook so far? Take a moment to subscribe to our FREE newsletter for incredible discounts, books giveaways, and VIP offers!

> http://www.connectionbooksclub.com/bonus/

All we need is your email, and you'll be set up to receive more of the eBooks you can't wait to read.

Affiliate Marketing via Blogging

If you already have a blog, then with a little bit of time, and with the right type of posts, you will be generating income passively in no time at all. This can be done through what is known as affiliate marketing, one of the most common types of passive income streams that many people start off by pursuing. As a blogger who is also an affiliate marketer, all you have to do is find products that you endorse, write about them while including links to buy the products, and get paid when your readers click on through and make a purchase based on your recommendation.

There are many types of affiliate marketing platforms out there and each offers a different method of compensation for their affiliate marketers. Amazon is once again a solid choice with Amazon Associates having the ability to link to any page on Amazon and receive a small commission that is typically a small percentage of the sale price of the item in question. There are literally hundreds of alternatives to Amazon Associates, however, with many keeping their focus to a particular niche. While finding the right affiliate platform for you might be somewhat time-consuming, the benefits will far outweigh the costs in the long term. Throughout your search, you should also be on the lookout for the right compensation model for you.

The pay per sale model is the compensation model that you will come across most often and it is the type of compensation that you are likely the most familiar with as well. Essentially, you receive a percentage of the sale price of each item that you help sell. In general, this type of compensation model is seen as the least beneficial to affiliate marketers and the most beneficial for sellers. This is because, as an affiliate marketer, your ability to make a sale is ultimately limited to the merchant's ability to seal the deal once they have left your website.

While not necessarily the fairest for affiliate marketers, this method of compensation still has the potential to generate a significant profit in certain scenarios. As such, it is important to take into account the specifics of the agreement in question, instead of simply refusing them all outright. Specifically, you will want to look for items with a high commission rate or, alternately, those that you find easier to sell. As with many types of sales, the general rule of thumb is that the items that are more lucrative to sell, will also be sold in a more competitive market.

Another common compensation method, pay per click compensation instead pays a small amount each time a viewer clicks through to the merchant's site. This is typically much easier to accomplish than a full-blown sale and, as such, typically pays much less as well. This method of compensation can often be seen as a middle ground between affiliate marketers and sellers because it relies on both equally in order to make a successful sale.

Finally, the pay per impression compensation method pays the least of all of the compensation methods because all you need to do is drive people to your site as normal and you are then compensated for every thousand which simply see the advertisement in question. This is the most beneficial arrangement for affiliate marketers as you get paid without viewers having to take any type of action.

Affiliate Marketing via Facebook

You can practice the affiliate marketing practices outlined in chapter 4 using Facebook, though your success rate will likely decrease as Facebook actively tries to keep posts related to advertising out of the standard news feed as much as possible. Instead, if you wish to promote affiliate products on Facebook, the best way to do so is by using Facebook's built in advertising options. Creating targeted Facebook advertisements is a great way to ensure that the people you are targeting are specifically interested in a specific hobby or interest. With their extreme access to data, studies show that Facebook targeting is up to 90 percent more accurate than its competitors.

To create an ad that you want to run on Facebook, you simply use the Facebook

Ads Manager which can be accessed at Facebook.com/Business. After ensuring your Ads Manager account is linked to your regular account you will want to create an ad campaign and start by choosing a goal for the advertisement in question. Advertising goals range in specificity but, in general, you are likely going to want to choose increase conversions on a website or send viewers to a website, though other options may apply.

The next step is likely the most important as it is where you determine just who you want to target with the advertisement in question. You will want to fill in as many of the given choices as possible because the more targeted your ad campaign is, the more likely it is that it is going to work properly. You will want to choose a location, the age of the targeted audience as well as their gender and any suggested interests they might have. You will also be able to include additional languages, connections, behaviors and categories you feel will be the most interested in your advertisements. Facebook provides a meter which will show just how targeted your overall results are.

Once the metrics for the advertising are set, you will then want to determine how much you are willing to spend on the advertising, which will likely be mostly based on how much you hope to make in terms of compensation. If you find the right margin between what you are making and what it is costing you, you will have a passive income stream that will require little more from you as long as it remains effective. You will also be able to determine the schedule for the advertisement which includes the start and end dates. With this information you will then be able to determine how much each click is worth to you personally or simply allow Facebook to determine the best value per click. From there it is only a matter of finalizing your choices and waiting for the clicks or impressions to start rolling in.

Affiliate Marketing via YouTube

When it comes to practicing affiliate marketing on YouTube, the most effective method is not to rely on YouTube advertising, but it is instead to go the other way and devote all of your time to actively promoting the niche of products you have chosen. Unlike in other marketing avenues, the genre of video product reviews is healthy enough to not need to be couched in any other type of content. In fact, short and to the point videos expressing the strengths and weaknesses of various products routinely rack up a million or more views when done properly. From there it is simply a matter of setting up a traditional affiliate program and putting a link to the item in question in your descriptions.

Creating a YouTube account is as easy as having a Google Account and going to YouTube.com to claim your page. From there it is important to post new content frequently so that you can build up an audience who expects new videos related to your niche. Think 3 or 4 to week to start as you want as many people to subscribe as possible.

When it comes to creating product review videos the first thing you will want to keep in mind is that they should always be less than 3 minutes in length. A majority of the interest in these videos comes from individuals who are looking for help making a buying decision in the moment. This means that they will almost certainly skip long videos for those that get right to the point. All of the pretenses is stripped out of this interaction, give the people what they want and you will be guaranteed to see results.

When it comes to discussing the item in question, it is important to make it clear what the factual strengths and weaknesses of the items in question are, without including your opinion as much as possible. Unless you back up your opinion with a fact about how much you used the product and in what conditions, your opinion is meaningless and will only eat up valuable seconds. Along those same lines, it is important to start with the most important information related to the products, including all of its major features. From there, if you still have time, you will want to work your way through lesser features that are still relevant, though you should never be obligated to fill time. Remember, a short video is better than a video that is exactly 3 minutes long with lots of filler.

After you have filmed the video, it is important to take the time to edit it in such a way that it keeps the momentum up throughout the video. While many people rely on static shots of products and a simple voice-over monolog, going a step further and including plenty of quick edits will ensure that people seek out your videos specifically, which will, in turn, lead to the results you are hoping for in the long term.

Enjoying your eBook so far? Take a moment to subscribe to our FREE newsletter for incredible discounts, books giveaways, and VIP offers!

- http://www.connectionbooksclub.com/bonus/

All we need is your email, and you'll be set up to receive more of the eBooks you can't wait to read.

Create a Webinar

If you are especially skilled in an area that you know other people would be interested in learning more about, then creating a webinar might be an easy way for you to create a passive income stream. When it comes to deciding on what topic you will create the webinar about, it is crucial that you only pick topics that you could be considered a master in. In order to sell a webinar successfully you need to be able to generate plenty of free content on the topic in question before asking people to pay for more, if you don't have access to this much information then creating a webinar can be a waste of time.

Once you have an idea of what you are interested in writing about, the next thing you will need to do is decide how you can best convey the information in question. This could be anything from a basic lecture where you literally stand in front of a camera and present the information, to something much more complex that requires charts, graphs and other generated elements to explain fully. It is important to have a clear idea of what your presentation will entail before you get started to ensure you have everything you need to produce a product that seems completely professional in every way.

Once you create your webinar you will need a place to host it online which means creating your own website as well. It is important that you populate this website with plenty of free content that demonstrates your mastery of the topic in question as fully as possible. Additionally, you will want to continue to update the website on a regular basis as an excuse to drive viewers to the site and also to prove you are still familiar with the current state of the topic in question.

Only by generating enough content that your readers become convinced of your mastery of the topic will then be willing to actually pay money to see what you keep behind the paywall.

When it comes to collecting payment for your webinar, it is important that you make the process as simple and painless as possible. This likely means using PayPal, and taking a hit on each purchase, but the ease of use will more than make up for the difference. Your goal should be to streamline this process to the point that your readers don't have time to rethink their purchase before it is already done and waiting for them to watch it. Remember, each hoop you make your customers jump through when it comes to buying your webinar is nothing but a chance for them to reconsider their purchase.

Finally, it is important to always offer a newsletter option for those who pay for your webinar as only by collecting their information will you be able to target future seminars at them directly. Those who have paid for one of your webinars are more than twice as likely to purchase the next so do what you can to ensure you get their information.

Sell Stock Photos

When it comes to selling stock photographs on websites such as iStockPhoto.com or ShutterStock.com the first thing you will need to consider is their selection process. Assuming your shots are up to the task, you will then make a percentage of each of your photos they sell. The average cut for new stock photographers is just 15 percent of each photo sold, though this can be improved to a solid 50/50 split if you sell enough pictures. As such, generating a reliable passive income stream with stock photos means creating photos that people want, and lots, and lots, of them.

If you are looking to maximize your profits from taking stock photos while minimizing your day-to-day effort it is important to decide if you are going to stick to the major sites which offer smaller percentages per photo or to smaller ones with a higher percentage of positive profit sharing and a smaller audience. While the easiest answer is to stick with the big 2, if you're pictures are of a somewhat lower quality, then many of the smaller sites offer a less stringent acceptance process which might be just what you are looking for.

If you are interested in taking stock photos, you don't need a photography degree but you will need a bit more of a robust skill set than simply turning a camera to auto. Take some time and do some research, both on your camera and one the best types of shots to cover the niche you are hoping to photograph. A few hours of study can lead to significant improvement.

When it comes to ensuring that you are taking the types of photographs that people actually want to buy, the first thing you will want to do is find the right niche which means that it is one with the right amount of supply and demand. Once you know what kind of pictures to take, you will want to view any potential pictures in the largest size possible to ensure there aren't any blemishes that are only visible once the photo reaches a certain scale.

Once you know your pictures are quality and error free, you next will be to post those using appropriate descriptions and keywords. While including too many keywords is only going to get your work ignored, it is important to include all of those that the picture could work for, including those that might be considered a counter-programing type choice. This is the only way you will get prospective buyers to your photo pages, make the most of it.

Along with being as descriptive as possible, it is important to always put some of your pictures into the free categories that most of these types of websites often provide. While this may seem as though you are simply giving money away, in reality it is best to think of it as advertising. People often start out in the free photo section before moving on to paid content and seeing your name there can give them an idea of where to start when looking for similar photographs.

Use Your Smartphone

As surprising as it might sound, there are currently numerous applications for smartphones that require very little of you in return for a steady, if modest revenue stream. While none of the following applications will lead to the type of passive income stream that you can one day live off of, they all require very little effort on your part beyond the use of your personal information. Remember, even if each of these applications only generates a few hundred dollars per year each, that is still nearly a thousand dollars that you made for doing basically nothing.

The Screenwise Trends Panel Application is the application related to Google's research branch. After you sign up all you have to do is to use the internet as you normally would and you are rewarded in a variety of ways including cash and gift cards. Additionally, if you install their information gathering products on 3 different devices you get an additional $3 per week as well. The goal of this application is to improve the development of future Google products and anyone with a computer, tablet or smartphone is eligible to participate.

The application for Media Insiders monitors your media use for the purposes of helping media companies understand the viewing habits of modern viewers. As with the Google application, all you need to do is download the application to your device and then view content as normal. Media Insider is only available to those with an Android OS on smartphones or tablets and a Windows operating system on PC. Media insider uses have the ability to earn a maximum of 200 points each week based on their viewing habits. In turn, those 200 points can be redeemed for $2 cash each week with the ability to turn in points becoming available with every 2,500 points. Additionally, if you earn 200 points for 13 weeks in a row you are given a bonus 1,000 points.

Survey Savvy is another application, though this one is only available to those living in the United States. Survey Savvy pays as much as $60 for putting its code on your device and includes smartphones, tablets and traditional computers. Additionally, Survey Savvy users also have the option of being entered into the running for survey participation, which can pay as much as $75 per survey. Additionally, you will earn $5 per month per device that you install their software on. You can also earn additional funds for referring friends into the system.

Finally, Perk TV is an application that pays out a specific number of points that can be eventually translated into cash just for watching videos from their database that they are being paid to increase the views for. These videos are typically only around 2 minutes. They also offer Amazon gift cards which pay out at a higher return per point than cash as well as the option to turn your points into bitcoins. What's more, there is nothing you actively need to do between videos meaning you can set it in motion and walk away while still earning.

Enjoying your eBook so far? Take a moment to subscribe to our FREE newsletter for incredible discounts, books giveaways, and VIP offers!

> http://www.connectionbooksclub.com/bonus/

All we need is your email, and you'll be set up to receive more of the eBooks you can't wait to read.

Create Evergreen Written Content

While blogging can lead to an amalgamation of a passive and active income stream, writing evergreen content specifically is a more passive income focused approach whereby you generate how-to content on popular information aggregation websites and then sell the ad space on those pages for a long term profit. Each of the major question answering platforms including Yahoo Answers, InfoBarrel, Quora , Squidoo, eHow and HubPages all offer differing amounts of a revenue sharing plan that typically scales based on how prolific you are in generating content and how popular your content ultimately ends up being.

While the totals will obviously vary between sites, a realistic estimate is that 50 articles could net you as much as $100 per month in completely passive income once the articles have been written. The best place to start when it comes to writing articles is in a niche that you are familiar with, especially if that niche seems somewhat barren on the readily available information front. Remember, if all you can bring to a topic is the depth of knowledge that 20 minutes of online searching can find, you might want to consider a different passive income stream instead.

Unlike when it comes to researching other types of passive income niches, when it comes to generating evergreen content, the more deserted a niche is when you get to it the better. If you can become the de facto source for the information on a given niche, then you will likely begin to see serious hits as long as the content you are creating is both accurate and easy for the average person to understand and put into use as needed. When generating content, it is important to take the time to create the types of keywords and search terms that people are generally going to use when searching for the topic in question.

Despite the name, keywords are more and more key phrases which is why it is important to start your keyword research by entering a common phrase related to the niche in question and see what comes up under the Google autofill options. This list of phrases will give you a good idea of what people are searching for when it comes to your niche and hopefully they will be phrases you can include seamlessly into your writing. The average key phrase is about 3 words and is the right mix of unique while still being common usage.

Instead of writing your content first and then looking for ways to get it to conform to the SEO specifications you are looking for, it is a better idea to start by working out an SEO strategy that will likely work for the content you want to generate and then simply generate it to the required specifications. Having an outline will likely make the actual writing process go easier as well, which in turn will make it easier for you to generate enough content to see a return on your time investment.

Become an Instagram Personality

There are currently more than 450 million users on Instagram each month with more than 25 percent of those using the service on a daily basis. This means that there is finally enough interest in the space that advertisers are starting to wonder how they can best monetize it. If you are looking to take advantage of this booming market then it is best to start by clearing defining yourself in the crowded Instagram space by, you guessed it, choosing a niche that is popular, but not too popular.

Your goal in this scenario is to generate enough interest in your content that you can maximize your number of followers in as little time as possible. In this instance followers directly equate to advertising dollars which are why it is important to do whatever you can to spread your reach as rapidly as possible. To start, you will want to ensure potential followers can find you by filling out your biography page in the appropriate way. You will want to start with personal details that will make you seem relatable to your niche, as well as information about the type of photos you post on a regular basis. From there you will want to include relevant key phrases as well as hashtags so searching for your content is as easy as possible.

Once you have made it easy for people to follow your work, you will want to ensure you are taking the best pictures possible based on the trends related to photographing your unique niche. You will want to take plenty of pictures and post them every single day, typically multiple times each day to give people a reason to follow you instead of just checking in on your work occasionally. If you don't know what types of pictures you should be taking, the best course of action is to simply try and seek out other individuals who are working in the same niche.

Getting an idea of what is popular in the niche is a great way to start you off in the right direction without actively copying the ideas of what other people are doing. The Instagram community can be surprisingly close-knit and if you start copying photo ideas someone is sure to notice. While you are gaining inspiration, it will also behoove you to leave feedback on the pages of the photographers you like and interact with the other followers who are there as well. This will help you grow in stature in the community as it will show you are there to do more than just making money based on page views.

Once you have reached 10,000 followers you can start reaching out to advertisers who are known to advertise on Instagram in your niche. You will need at least this many followers if you hope to set up an impression based ad-revenue stream that will reliably generate the types of results you are looking for. If you choose to go an affiliate route, it is important to not go overboard on the promotion and instead link it naturally into your daily postings in a way that is unobtrusive.

Become a YouTube Personality

After you have started a YouTube channel as described in chapter 6, you have a couple of different options when it comes to generating passive income with it. You might find it beneficial if you have generated other types of passive income content that you are looking to market or you may find it useful to instead go the more traditional route and create content that your niche might find relevant and/or humorous. When it comes to filling your channel with relevant content, you should aim for at least 2 videos per week as well as a regular posting schedule that your potential viewers will be able to rely on. Reliably creating content over the long term is the single most important part of creating a popular, and money making, YouTube channel.

Each video you post should also include the right keywords and key phrases that will get it noticed by members of your niche as well as an accurate and compelling description. Posting your videos without including these relevant facts is akin to shouting into a void; label your content the right way if you want anyone else to see it. When it comes to building an audience, you will want to make videos that are likely to generate a discussion among your followers. Interacting with your viewers is one of the best ways to keep them coming back and wanting to share your videos with your peers. Keep the conversations on track, however, as YouTube comment sections can devolve into dangerous places if not moderated properly.

When it comes to creating the type of content that people are interested in interacting with, the first thing that people are going to care about is how you present yourself.

YouTube celebrities are the modern day television stars and subscribers want to be able to connect to the people whose content they are regularly consuming. This means you want to be able to create a persona that you can stick with and then generate the type of content that you know people in the niche are going to respond positively towards.

After you have started building an audience you can turn on Google AdSense by looking for the monetization tab underneath the Ad heading. Google AdSense will pay you per impressions on your page as well as per clicks. The average video generates roughly 20 cents per click with the average of 1 percent click-through expected on each video. With these sorts or returns, it is either important to have a few extremely well-watched videos or numerous videos that each has a moderate number of hits.

YouTube channels with a larger number of subscribers are also able to garner a more equitable rate when it comes to advertising streams, and those whose channels really take off are then eligible for an additional tier of advertising whereby ads play prior to videos and each of these videos will pay you a small amount simply for each subscriber who views them.

Enjoying your eBook so far? Take a moment to subscribe to our FREE newsletter for incredible discounts, books giveaways, and VIP offers!

> http://www.connectionbooksclub.com/bonus/

All we need is your email, and you'll be set up to receive more of the eBooks you can't wait to read.

Become a Facebook Personality

While Facebook isn't the one-stop-shop for social media that it was several years ago, there is still plenty of money to be made there if you know where to look. Advertisers have been using Facebook for years which means it is relatively easy for anyone to make money there if they follow the right method of doing so. The first thing you need to do is to create a page that you are going to use to generate passive income that is separate from your personal page, while this may seem like a hassle, it will be more than worth it in the long run.

The first thing you will need to do should not surprise you, and that is find the niche you are interested in marketing content to and then filling your timeline with the type of content that you know will draw them to your page. Finding an underserved niche is much more difficult than in other scenarios due to Facebook's long history of popularity, so instead it is a better idea to stick with a niche you are familiar with and expressly target a subset of the niche. Advertisers on Facebook like to know exactly who they would be targeting with their advertisements and sticking to a subset of the niche will be enough to provide a specific target audience for them to market to.

Using Facebook to create a passive income stream is only one of the ways that Facebook can be used to contribute to passive income, the other is by using a business Facebook page to promote the other passive income inducing content that you have already created. Remember, posting to Facebook is essentially free marketing when done properly and many of the steps are the same. For example, regardless of how you plan to monetize your page, the first thing you are going to want to do is posting a constant stream of relevant information to your page so that people will "like" it. If you are going to include promotional content, a good rule of thumb is that 1 promotional post for every 10 regular posts is tolerable to readers.

Once you have developed a reputation for posting niche specific content, the next thing you will want to do is get your community primed and ready to interact with your content on a regular basis by creating discussions or polls for your followers to interact with. The amount of interaction that you have with your community is going to directly affect how much you can charge for your marketing services. Additionally, you will want to interact with other related Facebook pages to help get the word out about your page and get it circulating within the community, the more you go out of your way to interact with all facets of the niche community the better.

Once you have a large following all you need to do is turn on AdSense for the page or consider selling Facebook Ad space to companies that target your niche. You can realistically expect around 5 cents for click through and 20 cents per thousand impressions if you can reach 50,000 likes and prove a high community interaction rate.

Peer-to-Peer Real Estate Investment

Paying for someone else to remodel a home has always been an attractive passive income stream for those in the know and these days it is easier than ever to meet individuals looking for a loan for the purpose of real estate investment. Over the past few years, a number of peer-to-peer (P2P) real estate investment websites have popped up offering both short term and long term loan options for those interested in buying and fixing up a property without the cash on hand to pay for it themselves.

Investing in these types of loans is often referred to as Trust Deed investing which means the investor is a private source of capital which is then loaned to the borrower. This investment is secured by a Trust Deed, hence the name and is the same regardless of which P2P lending platform you decide to use.

P2P real estate loans often have a number of benefits when it compared with more traditional bank loans, the first of which is that they are much easier for those seeking loans to qualifying for. They are also often much less rigid in terms of guidelines than traditional loans and often go through in a matter of hours, not weeks or months. They are also ideal for those looking to generate passive income streams because they don't require the investment of the full price of the property as with real world transactions. Instead, investors are able to invest the amount they are comfortable with and a clear idea of the repayment terms they can expect.

As with any other type of real estate investment, it is important to have a clear idea of the risks and benefits associated with the property in question. To that end, it is important to have a basic understanding of what the After Repair Value (ARV) of any property you are looking at is going to be. ARV can be thought of as the amount the property is going to be worth once the project is fully finished. This amount needs to be enough to cover the proposed costs of purchasing the property as well as renovations with enough left over to turn a profit for the person who is working on the property.

While theoretically this is only important to the person looking for the loan, if you hope to see a speedy return on your investment you need to be confident the project will come to fruition. Aside from ensuring the project is viable, you will also want to look at the plan the borrower has for the completion of the project as well as the tools and resources they have at their disposal. Finally, you will always want to ensure the property has been inspected by a competent individual to prevent surprises from popping up later on in the process. All told, if you find an A rated loan investment you can realistically expect around a 6 percent return on investment which is a fair yield in this type of market, especially at lower investment amounts.

Other Types of Peer to Peer Lending

While P2P real estate investing has its own challenges, there are also many other types of P2P lending scenarios which mean that anyone with $50 and the time to find the right loan can put their money to work generating a passive income. Unlike other types of P2P services, P2P loans are completely on the level and backed by the Securities and Exchange Commission which means they are as safe as any other type of investment. The largest P2P lending site is LendingClub.com which has issued nearly 300,000 loans for a total of nearly 3 billion dollars.

In order to become a borrower, applicants must provide their debt-to-income ratio, credit score and credit history as well as be a permanent resident of the United States. All of this information is used to assign the borrower a rating which equates to their overall level of risk. Borrowers are then allowed to ask to borrow up to $35,000.

Potential loaners are then free to browse the website and fund part or all of a loan that a borrower is looking for. The return on these investments can be anywhere from 6 percent of the total all the way up to 26 percent depending on how much of a risk the borrower has been assessed as being. The terms are then specified based on the amount borrowed and you have nothing else to do but wait for the return on your investment to manifest itself. Unlike many other types of passive income streams this stream can produce significant returns but only if you invest accordingly.

While the return can be greater than or equal to various other forms of investing, it is actually taxed at a different rate than stock market returns in that it is considered a form of income. This means you will be paying taxes on the money before you invest it and again on the return on your investment.

Additionally, despite having been around for a decade, P2P lending is still not legal in every state which means you must live in Montana, Mississippi, Colorado, California, Arkansas, Arizona, Alabama, Delaware, Connecticut, Illinois, Idaho, Iowa, Indiana, Missouri, Minnesota, New Jersey, New Hampshire, Nevada, Nebraska, New York, Michigan, Kentucky, Kansas, Georgia, Florida, Louisiana, Hawaii, Massachusetts, Maine, Oregon, Oklahoma, South Dakota, South Carolina, Tennessee, Rhode Island, Washington, Virginia, Wisconsin, West Virginia, Wyoming, Vermont, Utah, Texas in order to seriously consider this passive income stream.

Before you invest in a P2P lending platform it is important to take into account your own tolerance for risk in regards to potential investments. This means it is important to take into account finding a loan that offers a 20 percent or more return on the initial invest. Specifically, the borrower in question is forced to pay a higher rate because they have the likely default on loans before or, at the very least, have a severe habit of late payments. Keep in mind what you are getting into, and always invest responsibly.

Enjoying your eBook so far? Take a moment to subscribe to our FREE newsletter for incredible discounts, books giveaways, and VIP offers!

> http://www.connectionbooksclub.com/bonus/

All we need is your email, and you'll be set up to receive more of the eBooks you can't wait to read.

Run a Comparison Site

Running a comparison based price aggregation website is a covert way to market products of your affiliates without even having to create any content yourself. Comparison based price aggregation websites are a great way to create a passive income stream because while they are extremely common for certain types of products, most niches have yet to latch on to a particular site for its products of choice.

The first step to creating this type of site is finding the right products to list which mean tracking down a niche that has a lot of products all competing for market and mind share. You are going to want to find products that contain a lot of similar sounding features that actually can produce differing results for the subset of consumers who know how to use them properly. The goal should be to provide the type of side by side analysis that it will difficult for the consumer to find without a considerable time commitment. To minimize the amount of upkeep you have to do to the site, ensure that new products in the field only come out once or twice per year.

After you determine your niche you will want to consider various affiliate marketing platforms that work with companies related to the niche in question. Remember, you are going to want as many products, which means as many merchants as possible. If you can't find any that provide you with the breadth of clientele that you are looking for, the next best choice is to instead go with the Amazon affiliate program as you are guaranteed to find the amount of differing products that you are looking for.

Once you have set up your affiliate items, you will want to present them in such a way that all of the various strengths and weaknesses that consumers might care about are clearly displayed without clearly ranking them in a way that implies one is inherently better than any other. The goal should be to present the information as matter-of-factly as possible, remember, you are still trying to sell all of the products listed, even if some are more lackluster than others. Your job as an affiliate is to simply generate interest in a product and, most likely, generate a click through in the process it is up to the merchant to sell the less than perfect products.

When it comes to driving content to your site, the first thing you will want to consider is your Search Engine Optimization, which shouldn't be hard based on the content of the site, keep in mind that key phrases are now more important than keywords. Additionally, you may want to flesh out the content of your site by including reviews, properly sourced, from major names in the niche related to the products in question. It is important to always repost these reviews to your own site, including attribution, and never link away from your site as you never know if you can trust the potential customer to come back once they have left.

Run a Lead Capture Site

A lead generation site is a site that makes money by connecting potential customers with relevant businesses. This typically comes in the form email addresses, though the more information you are able to extract from users the better. To create a lead generation site, the first thing you are going to have to do is find the right niche to capture leads from. The niche in question, in this case, can often be of a much different sort than you would cater to in many of these other passive income scenarios as you don't need to worry about marketing to them directly. This means you can consider geographic region, many other types of demographics, or household income as all viable candidates.

Before you become too involved in the lead capture site building process it is important to look into the general requirements that companies like the one you are creating have when it comes to the niche you have selected. Those from some areas who wish to work in lead generation require a license to work in the real estate or mortgage industries at both the federal and state level. If you are unsure about the requirements related to your niche, seek out your local chamber of commerce for more information.

Once you are ready to build your site you need to turn your attention to a way to create a system of generating leads that also allows you to collect as much personal information as possible. This means you need to find a way that you can reliably corral people to your site and make them want to provide you with their information. The best way to do this is to offer up content that has value to your visitors in exchange for their email address. Then, you simply ask them for some ancillary information as part of the checkout process. The key to doing this successfully is to simply relate it back to the niche in hand which will ensure your collection rate is as high as possible.

Once you have a significant number of leads generated and, more importantly, a system that has a proven record of the content generation you can start reaching out to businesses who you know target consumers in the demographics that you have collected. While you can do research and reach out to clients individually, a more effective solution is likely to create a landing page for potential clients who can then take a look at your operation for themselves before they decide if they want to use your services further.

As you gather information on individuals in specific demographics, it is important that you not only store this information but take the extra time and effort to find an effective database storage solution that works for you. While this will initially be a complicated process, the amount of time you save when it comes to pulling leads in the future will more than make up for the initial development costs. The more search parameters you include the better, as you want to be able to generate as many different lists from the same data as possible.

Run a Website that Sells a Real-World Service

In this passive income scenario, you create a website that aggregates a specific type of service in a hyper-specific region. For example, you could call a number of lawn care professionals who all work for themselves in your area and convince them to let you put their information on your site in exchange for a small percentage of the total work completed. While asking for only 5 percent in exchange for marketing and connecting those who need work with those to do it may seem generous, it is important to take a moment and think about how costly certain types of work can quickly end up being.

When it comes to choosing the right service niche it is important to consider the area you are targeting and consider what type of services it has a higher than average demand for. From there it is simply a matter of finding one that is necessary but not urgent as people are still likely to call someone themselves for things like heating, cooling, electrical and plumbing issues. By contrast, maintenance jobs can often be sought after online because there is time to value shop and read reviews.

After you have decided on a niche you are going to want to build an eye-catch website and load it with a few samples so that the individual business owners can see just what they are signing up for if they agree to your proposition. One particular advantage of this particular passive income scenario is that if you choose a narrow enough sub-niche then you should be able to practically guarantee that those in your area will find your site first when it comes time to fill their service specific needs. It is still important to capitalize on this SEO boon, however, and include lots of location and service based key phrases that people are likely to type in when they are in need of the service in question.

To see better results, it may be best to forgo online marketing entirely and instead look into a small advertisement in the local newspaper or even physical leaflets left at local coffee shops or stores that sell niche adjacent supplies. While it might seem old fashioned, in reality, it is just targeted marketing, the more that your potential customers see your name and website the more likely they are to think of it when they are finally in need of your services.

While requiring relatively little from you in terms of post-startup effort, this type of website is more of an official business than many of the other passive income scenarios discussed in the preceding chapters which means that in order to protect yourself and ensure you are paid for your services you will want to form an LLC for a few hundred dollars to ensure that you cannot be held liable in case anything goes wrong. Having your own company will also make it easier to hire an attorney to ensure that you are paid for the clients you find for the individuals in question.

Enjoying your eBook so far? Take a moment to subscribe to our FREE newsletter for incredible discounts, books giveaways, and VIP offers!

> http://www.connectionbooksclub.com/bonus/

All we need is your email, and you'll be set up to receive more of the eBooks you can't wait to read.

Run a Drop Shipping Business

In this passive income scenario, you build a website selling a specific product or group of products and then outsource the fulfillment of every order to a third party who handles product acquisition, storage and fulfillment responsibilities. While the profits from this type of passive income website are likely going to be less robust than some others because the fulfilment company is going to take a large portion of the total profits, the amount of work you have to do extends no further than creating and marketing your website as you see fit.

When it comes to finding the right items to sell, you first want to consider products for your niche that are easy to ship and are likely to always arrive intact as you will still be in charge of customer service and you will have no way of ensuring that proper care is taken with each delivery. Once you have an idea of what you want to sell, you will need to do research into companies that dropship the items in question. It is important to have realistic expectations during this step as the pool of items that are available to be sold in this way might be shallower than you first hope.

When it comes to finding the right drop shipping company, you will want to ensure you are working with a wholesaler and not a retailer as you will never be able to make a profit on retail prices. You will also want to look into drop shipping companies that create items versus those that buy and sell as the price differences can be significant. Remember, even if you are saving a few dollars per unit shipped that will add up quickly, do your homework and you will see the financial rewards.

When setting up a drop shipping business your best bet is to not spring for your own website which will need much more marketing to begin seeing real success and to instead choose a merchant platform that caters to the niche you are working with. There are countless niche specific marketing platforms, a little digging should help you find yours, and though you might want to choose an adjacent platform instead as it will help to be competing with as few similar products as possible.

Once you have chosen a platform you will want to do everything you can to set yourself apart from other similar stores as much as possible. Ensure that the pictures you are using for all of the products in question are of a high quality and show the product from numerous angles including at least one picture of the item in use. Likewise, once you make a sale it is important to have a realistic idea of just when the product is going to reach the customer. The best way to always ensure customer satisfaction in this instance is to simply quote each customer a shipping time of 2 days more than what the drop shipping company tells you to cut down on customer complaints.

Organize Public Domain Information

In this passive income scenario, you create a website that aggregates some form of public domain content that people often need access to and then sell click-through and impression based ad space once the quality of your content aggregation has generated a significant amount of traffic. Public domain content is anything including music, pictures and reams and reams of text, whose author copyright has expired which means that anyone can use if for any purpose. Additionally, many people also create copyright free work that is instantly added to the public domain.

When creating the site, it is important to stick to a specific niche of content as it will make it easier for you to rise through the SEO ranks. The only way you are going to reliably make money through this passive income scenario is if you are on the first page of Google search results which means when looking for a niche it is important to find one whose search results are not locked up by professionals. Additionally, the content in question should be easy to locate with enough ads to make it worth your time but without so many that it drives users away.

When creating a website whose primary function is to allow people to download content from it, the most important thing you need to keep in mind is that your site needs to look as professional as possible. If potential users come to your site and feel as though there might be a virus attached to the files they are looking for they will leave in a hurry. A professional site promises a comprehensive search function and should include a verification of file accuracy and safety, anything less will never generate the traffic that you need to turn a profit.

When it comes to acquiring public domain content, the first place you should consider is PublicDomainReview.org which collects a wide variety of public domain content as well as resources for finding your own. Likewise, a Twitter search for such content can be surprisingly fruitful though you will want to verify the content for yourself before using it. When it comes to finding the right content it is important to dig deeper than the first dozen or so music files that you come across as only by hosting unique content can you start to guarantee truly that your site will begin to gain traction in the niche in question.

While you may be tempted to try and sell the content you are hosting, the fact that the content is in the public domain will certainly work against you. This fact can be circumvented, however, if you offer up a lower quality version of the work in question for free, while also offering a higher quality group of related content, easily package and ready to go in exchange for a small fee. Be aware just how much hosting fees are going to cost you, however, as larger files, downloaded frequently, can quickly get expensive.

Dear Reader,

Connection Books Club wants to thank you for the purchase of one of our many informative eBooks! We hope you enjoyed your purchase and we want to invite you to join our club.

When you subscribe to our FREE club, you'll receive regular newsletters and incredible discounts on our bestselling books! Connection Books Club makes reading easy, giving you the content you want, at a price you can't believe. All that it takes to enroll in our FREE book club is your email. We'll send you the latest business and personal development news and highlight the newest books that are ready for you to enjoy.

> ➤ http://www.connectionbooksclub.com/bonus/

As part of your subscription, we're giving you a FREE download of one of our favorite eBooks, *Money Management: Learn How to Organize Your Financial Life and Invest in Your Future*. This eBook covers many financial situations, such as lowering interest rates and exploring options surrounding bankruptcy, helping you determine the best financial action for you.

Money management may be difficult for some people, but with your FREE copy of *Money Management: Learn How to Organize Your Financial Life and Invest in Your Future,* you'll learn the skills and information you need to make the best decisions to secure your financial future. The strategies contained in this eBook, designed for the everyday person, offering easy to follow steps and money saving tips.

Understanding money and how to make it works for you is important and with this eBook, you'll learn what you need to know to start building your financial security. Here are the top 5 reasons for reading *Money Management: Learn How to Organize Your Financial Life and Invest in Your Future*:

1. The strategies in this book are designed to help real people achieve their financial goals.
2. Explore different options for retirement.
3. Discover hacks for navigating the grocery store's subtle spending traps.
4. Inform yourself about how you might be able to get away with paying less than you owe on credit cards and other outstanding debts.
5. Experience a feeling of newfound freedom when you understand that you have every ability to live a life of financial stability.

➢ Get your copy here:
   http://www.connectionbooksclub.com/bonus/

The benefits of receiving this eBook for FREE are endless! Take control of your finances and start living the life you want.

By subscribing to Connection Books Club, not only will you get incredible discounts, our FREE welcome gift eBook, and a regular newsletter, but you'll also get the opportunity to receive FREE eBooks! Subscribers are invited to share reviews of the eBooks they've read, earning new titles at no cost! All it takes to enroll is your email.

http://www.connectionbooksclub.com/bonus/

Discounts and free eBooks are just a click away! Enter your email for VIP access to new books, incredible deals and money saving options, and even free giveaways! And don't forget, by signing up today for Connection Books Club, you'll receive the incredible eBook *Money Management: Learn How to Organize Your Financial Life and Invest in Your Future* for FREE!

Connection Books Club is excited to have you join our ranks of subscribers. We hope you enjoy your FREE eBook and all the great reading coming your way soon!

http://www.connectionbooksclub.com/bonus/

Wrap up: Passive Income overview

Thank for making it through to the end of *Passive Income: 20 Ideas and Strategies to Start an Online Business That Make a Passive Income for You Every Day* let's hope it was informative and was able to provide you with all of the tools you need to achieve your goals both in the near term and for the months and years ahead. Remember, just because you've finished this book doesn't mean there isn't anything left to learn on the topic. Becoming an expert at something is a marathon, not a sprint, slow and steady wins the race.

The next step is to stop reading already and put some of the passive income generation scenarios outlined above to work for you as soon as possible. Remember, regardless of which scenario you pursue it is important to consider carefully your niche and find one that has enough interest to ensure it will be worthwhile while at the same time not being too overcrowded and competitive. Take your time, find the right niche, and generate the passive income you have always dreamed of, it really is that simple.

If you've enjoyed this book, I'd greatly appreciate if you could leave an honest review on Amazon.

Reviews are very important to us authors, and it only takes a minute to post.

Thank you

www.ingramcontent.com/pod-product-compliance
Lightning Source LLC
Chambersburg PA
CBHW070412190526
45169CB00003B/1223